Sand warms up faster than water. Therefore, the air above the sand warms up faster than the air above water as well. As the warm air over the beach rises, cooler winds blow in from the sea. That's why you can almost always feel a breeze on the beach. So the next time you're looking for a windy spot to fly a kite, try the beach.

This diagram shows the movement of warm air and cool air in a cycle. This is called convection. You can see how the process on the shore is the opposite at night as the land cools off.

# CONVECTION

**Sea breeze**

**Land breeze**

# CHAPTER TWO

# KNOW YOUR STREAMS

The **atmosphere** is a busy place. It's an ocean of air that is always moving. Within this atmospheric sea there are "rivers of air," called **currents**. When currents move at high speed over long distances they are called jets. Jets play an important role in the weird weather we have down here on Earth. These jets form in the part of Earth's atmosphere called the **tropopause**. The tropopause is where the **stratosphere** and the **troposphere** meet.

# THE WEATHER REPORT

# Jet Stream Steering the Winds!

Edited by Joanne Randolph

SUNDAY

MONDAY

TUESDAY

WEDNESDAY

THURSDAY

FRIDAY

SATURDAY

This edition published in 2018 by:
Enslow Publishing, LLC.
101 W. 23rd Street, Suite 240
New York, NY 10011

Additional materials copyright © 2018 by Enslow Publishing, LLC

**Cataloging-in-Publication Data**

Names: Randolph, Joanne, editor.
Title: Jet stream steering the winds! / edited by Joanne Randolph.
Description: New York : Enslow Publishing, 2018 | Series: The weather report |
Includes bibliographical references and index. | Audience: Grades 3-5.
Identifiers: ISBN 9780766090194 (library bound) | ISBN 9780766090170 (pbk.) | ISBN 9780766090187 (6 pack)
Subjects: LCSH: Winds--Juvenile literature. | Weather--Juvenile literature. |
Climatology--Juvenile literature.
Classification: LCC QC931.4 J48 2018 | DDC 551.51/8—dc23
Printed in the United States of America

**To Our Readers:** We have done our best to make sure all website addresses in this book were active and appropriate when we went to press. However, the author and the publisher have no control over and assume no liability for the material available on those websites or on any websites they may link to. Any comments or suggestions can be sent by email to customerservice@enslow.com.

**Photo Credits:** Cover, p. 1 mirounga/Shutterstock.com (wind turbines), solarseven/Shutterstock.com (weather symbols); series logo NPeter/Shutterstock.com; interior pages background image, back cover, Sabphoto/Shutterstock.com; pp. 3, 28, 30, 32 Igor Zh./Shutterstock.com; pp. 4, 8, 18, 24 NASA/GSFC/LaRC/JPL, MISR Team; p. 5 Education Images/Universal Images Group/Getty Images; p. 6 Hero Images/Getty Images; p. 7 Designua/Shutterstock.com; p. 9 Anita Potter/Shutterstock.com; p. 11 Claus Lunau/Science Photo Library/Getty Images; p. 13 © AP Images; p. 15 Dan Craggs/Wikimedia; p. 16 BSIP SA/Alamy Stock Photo; p. 19 Monica Schroeder/Science Source; p. 20 Justin Sullivan/Getty Images; p. 22 Anadolu Agency/Getty Images; p. 25 Keystone/Hulton Archive/Getty Images; p. 26 mattscutt/RooM/Getty Images.

**Article Credits:** "What Makes the Wind?" *Click*; Gabriel Susca-Lopata and Peg Lopata, "Know Your Streams," *Odyssey*.

All articles © by Carus Publishing Company. Reproduced with permission.

All Cricket Media material is copyrighted by Carus Publishing Company, d/b/a Cricket Media, and/or various authors and illustrators. Any commercial use or distribution of material without permission is strictly prohibited. Please visit http://www.cricketmedia.com/info/licensing2 for licensing and http://www.cricketmedia.com for subscriptions.

# CONTENTS

# CHAPTER ONE

# WHAT MAKES THE WIND?

Wind is moving air. It can move so gently that you barely feel it. Or it can blow so hard that it knocks down trees.

You can make air move. Hold your hand in front of your mouth and blow. Can you feel air pushing against your hand? But what makes the air outside move?

The sun!

The sun powers a process called **convection**. This means that heat from the sun warms Earth's surface, which then warms the air above it. Warm air is lighter than cold air, so the warmed air floats up to the sky. As the warm air rises, cooler, heavier air rushes in to take its place. That air

Windy days are great days to fly kites. It is often windier along the shore since the air over the water and the air over the land can be different temperatures.

is, in turn, warmed and rises, while the air farther away from the surface loses its heat and sinks to fill the space. All that moving air is wind!

You might have noticed that some places are windier than others. Did you ever wonder why? One reason is that the sun doesn't heat places equally.

Have you ever walked barefoot on a sandy beach on a sunny summer day? The sand can get so hot it burns your feet, while the ocean stays nice and cool.

The beach is usually windy because of the cool sea air. It's the perfect place to play with a kite or pinwheel.

Thermosphere

Mesosphere

Stratosphere

Troposphere

This diagram shows the layers of the atmosphere and which ones are closer and farther away from Earth's surface.

## SUPER JETS

Jet streams are the biggest and fastest of the jets. They are like giant ribbons of eastward-moving air (or "westerly" wind) that often stretches all the way around Earth. They tend to run from west to east, partly due to Earth's rotation.

Jet streams are a few miles thick vertically and a few hundred miles wide horizontally. A jet stream doesn't stay in one spot. It moves northward and southward, and in many places it splits into two distinct branches. A jet stream doesn't travel in a straight line either. It curves like a snake of air moving across the planet. When and where a jet stream goes depends on the season, where low and high pressure systems are, and the temperature of the air. Jet streams are more active during winter.

The jet stream winds are moving pretty quickly. They tend to be more than 100 miles (161 kilometers) per hour (mph/kmh). The strongest winds in the jet stream often go faster than 200 mph (322 kmh). And once in a while, in some places, the winds approach nearly 300 mph (483 kmh). In comparison, hurricane winds's maximum speed are around 200 mph. The speed of the jet streams are greater where temperature differences between air masses are greatest.

# POLAR JETS AND SUBTROPICAL JETS

The northern and southern **hemispheres** both have two jet streams. The polar jets are near the poles and are the biggest and fastest jets. Polar jets tend to be between 4⅓ and 7½ miles (7 and 12 km) above sea level. Each hemisphere also has **subtropical** jets. These are weaker than the polar jets and much higher above sea level. These jet streams are found between 6 and 10 miles (10 and 16 km) above sea level. Both jets on the northern hemisphere are stronger than those in the southern hemisphere.

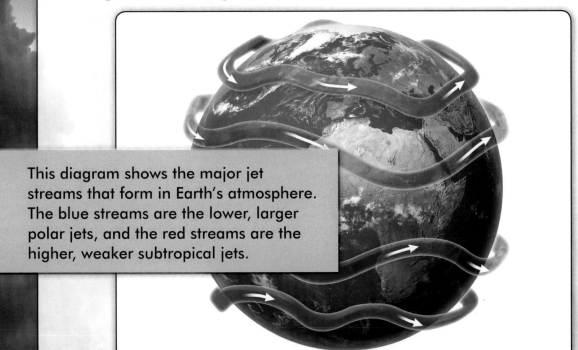

This diagram shows the major jet streams that form in Earth's atmosphere. The blue streams are the lower, larger polar jets, and the red streams are the higher, weaker subtropical jets.

## DRIVING THE WINDS

Fortunately for us, strong jet stream winds occur several miles above the surface of Earth. But they still affect us down here, bringing all kinds of catastrophic weather. For example, there was a major windstorm in Madison, Wisconsin, on October 26, 2010. Gusts of more than 70 mph (113 kmh) wreaked havoc. "This storm was tied to an incredibly strong jet stream—the strongest we've seen in years—that came racing across the Pacific Ocean a week before the storm," says Dr. Jon Martin, Chair of the Department of Atmospheric and Oceanic Sciences at the University of Wisconsin-Madison. "The jet stream was made so incredibly strong (wind speeds near 200 mph [322 kmh] at 6 miles [10 km] above the ground!) by its interaction with super typhoon Megi in the west Pacific Ocean. Megi was slammed up against the jet stream, and several days later that jet stream spawned this big windstorm."

The jet stream can also cause certain weather to get "stuck" in a particular area. In 2012, Britain experienced a lot of flooding because of the polar jet. Typically, the jet shifts northward in the summer months, but in 2012 it stayed over the area, causing more rain than usual.

This photograph captures the strong windstorm that hit Marshfield, Wisconsin, in 2010. The stop sign looks blurry because it is being moved so much by the wind.

## THE LOWLY JET

Air currents near the surface, up to a couple of thousand feet (hundreds of meters) above the surface, also play an important role in weather. One of these currents, called a low-level jet, is often involved in dramatic weather in the central United States and is partly responsible for the tornadoes in Tornado Alley, a popular term for the area in the United States where the most tornadoes occur. During the early spring, a low-level air stream can develop and bring warm, moist air from the Gulf of Mexico northward into the Great Plains states, such as Kansas and Oklahoma. The moisture and warm air from this low-level jet are like fuel for some of the severe thunderstorms that break out in the Plains during the spring. Some of these severe storms then go on to produce tornadoes.

Other low-level air currents can also move large amounts of moisture thousands of miles. Called "atmospheric rivers," they are similar to low-level jets. One, known as the Pineapple Express, carries moisture from near Hawaii all the way to the United States West Coast. The Express doesn't always run, though. Like many low-level jets, it only happens during certain conditions. Water from the Pineapple Express brought record rainfall and severe floods to the Pacific Northwest states in November 2006.

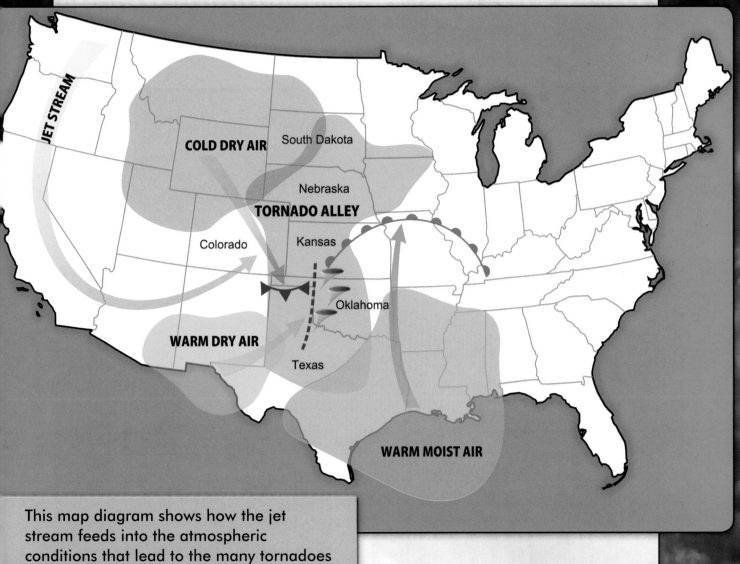

JET STREAM

COLD DRY AIR

South Dakota

Nebraska

**TORNADO ALLEY**

Colorado

Kansas

Oklahoma

**WARM DRY AIR**

Texas

**WARM MOIST AIR**

This map diagram shows how the jet stream feeds into the atmospheric conditions that lead to the many tornadoes in the region called Tornado Alley.

15

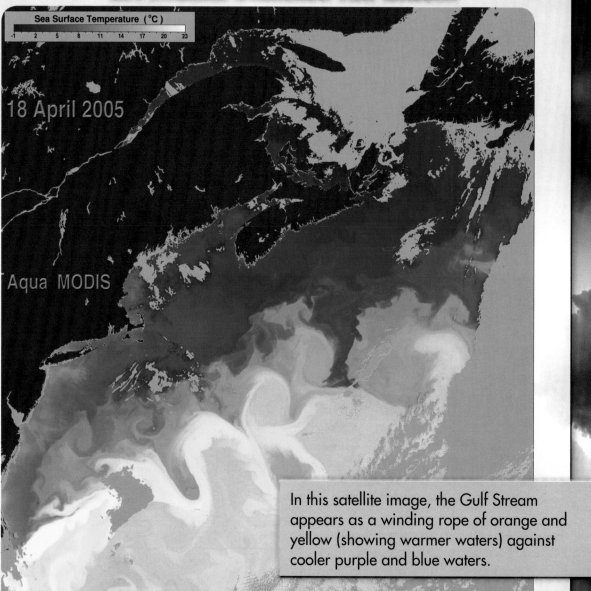

Sea Surface Temperature (°C)
-1    2    5    8    11    14    17    20    23

18 April 2005

Aqua MODIS

In this satellite image, the Gulf Stream appears as a winding rope of orange and yellow (showing warmer waters) against cooler purple and blue waters.

# THE GULF STREAM

The Gulf Stream gets lots of publicity because it affects hurricanes in the United States. It's not a stream in the air, like a jet stream, but a stream in the waters of the Atlantic Ocean. "Since the Gulf Stream is a current of very warm water at the ocean surface, hurricanes almost always strengthen when they travel over the Gulf Stream," says Jon Martin, a meteorology professor at University of Wisconsin-Madison. "The water vapor provides fuel for hurricanes like gasoline provides fuel for a car."

# CHAPTER THREE

# CLIMATE CHANGE AND THE STREAMS

Some scientists say **global warming**, also known as **climate** change, is already affecting the major atmospheric and water streams, while others think it is too soon to tell. Global warming is the gradual increase of Earth's temperature due to the greenhouse effect, which traps heat inside Earth's atmosphere and is caused by increased pollution and carbon dioxide in the air.

Dr. Joseph Kidston at the Climate Change Research Centre at the University of New South Wales says, "Global warming has caused the atmospheric jet streams to move away from the equator and towards the poles slightly, especially in the Southern Hemisphere." But Tom

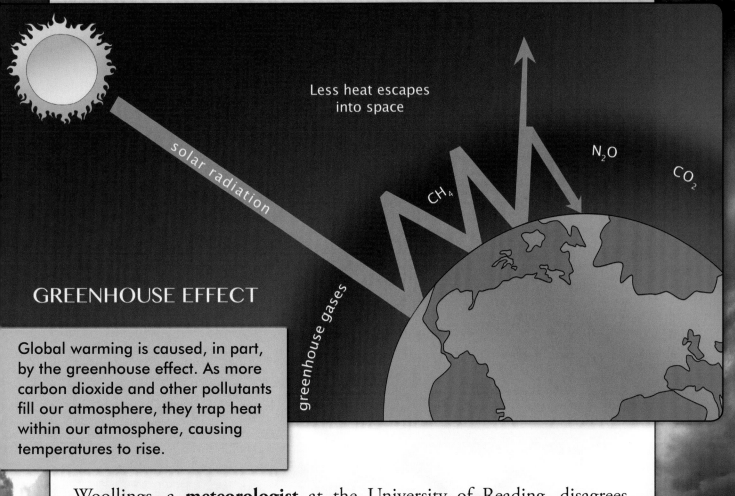

## GREENHOUSE EFFECT

solar radiation

Less heat escapes into space

greenhouse gases

$CH_4$

$N_2O$

$CO_2$

Global warming is caused, in part, by the greenhouse effect. As more carbon dioxide and other pollutants fill our atmosphere, they trap heat within our atmosphere, causing temperatures to rise.

Woollings, a **meteorologist** at the University of Reading, disagrees. "Global warming has probably not yet affected the jet or Gulf streams," he says. "The atmospheric jets vary so much from year to year that it's too early to see if [global warming] is causing this [movement] or if it is just natural variability."

19

California has been dealing with massive droughts for years. This lake, Lake Oroville, is nearly dry, as are many other California lakes and rivers.

Forecasts indicating what will happen to the streams with continued warming are not certain either.

According to Jian Lu, a research scientist at the Center for Land-Ocean-Atmosphere Studies at George Mason University, "The jet stream will rise up both vertically and pole-ward due to global warming." Joseph Kidston agrees, but he thinks the magnitude of the future shift is uncertain, because scientists don't really understand why the shift is occurring. "However, if it continues as it's been going over the last few decades," he says, "it has the potential to cause widespread changes in rainfall, particularly in the mid-latitudes where the majority of the world's population lives."

Lu thinks the shifting of the jets will also be accompanied by other changes in the atmosphere, which will "lead to an expansion of subtropical dry areas and impact the availability of water in the southwestern United States, Southern Europe, and Mediterranean Africa." The atmospheric changes will also lead to warmer, wetter weather in northern countries.

Woollings says the Gulf Stream is very stable and unlikely to be much affected by climate change. However, he says the Gulf Stream affects a large **circulation** of water in the Atlantic that keeps Europe

Climate change is a global problem.
Here, world leaders attend the United
Nations Climate Change Conference
held in Marrakech, Morocco, in 2016.

relatively mild, considering how far north it is. "This circulation, which is way too large to be called a jet, is expected to weaken under climate change, but there is strong agreement between climate models that it will not stop completely," he says. "This weakening might partly offset the warming expected over Europe, but not enough to reverse the trend and make Europe become cooler instead of warmer."

<br>

# CHAPTER FOUR

# USING THE JET STREAMS

The first person to study the jet streams was a Japanese meteorologist named Wasaburo Oishi. He was studying winds above Mt. Fuji in the 1920s. The name "jet stream" wasn't used back then, though. It was first called that by a German meteorologist in 1939. World War II pilots paid attention to jet streams, too. They noticed it made a difference in how long it took to fly to Japan if they were fighting against the jet stream. On the flip side, it sped things up on the way home.

One of the first times the jet streams were put to use was during World War II as pilots noticed flying in the stream slowed their trip to Japan but sped up the return trip.

25

Airlines use the jet streams as they plan and schedule flights to destinations around the world.

Airlines and pilots today pay close attention to the jet stream as well so they can plan flights and create schedules. When a plane flies into a jet stream, it uses more fuel, which is more expensive for the airline. On the other hand, when the plane flies with the jet stream, the wind pushes it along, saving the airline fuel and money. And flying in or out of a jet stream may cause the shaking motion often felt on flights known as **turbulence**.

Obviously, meteorologists today study the jet stream as they look at all the data that helps them predict the weather. The jet streams aren't just a lot of wind—they are useful!

# GLOSSARY

**atmosphere**  The blanket of gases surrounding a planet.

**circulation**  The movement back and forth or around something, such as warm and cold water moving back and forth.

**climate**  The kind of weather an area has over a long period of time.

**convection**  The movement casued by hotter, less dense gas or liquid to rise and colder, more dense gas or liquid to fall, which results in heat transfer.

**currents**  Bodies of water or air that are moving in a specific direction.

**global warming**  The gradual increase of Earth's temperature due to the greenhouse effect, which traps heat inside Earth's atmosphere and is caused by increased pollution and carbon dioxide in the air.

**hemisphere**  Half of a sphere.

**meteorologist** A scientist who studies weather patterns and data and makes predictions about future weather.

**stratosphere** The layer of Earth's atmosphere above the troposphere and below the mesosphere.

**subtropical** Relating to places just north or south of the tropics.

**tropopause** The part of Earth's atmosphere where the stratosphere and the troposphere meet.

**troposphere** The lowest level of Earth's atmosphere, which extends from the surface to between 4 and 6 miles (6½ and 10 km) above the surface.

**turbulence** The shaking motion felt on flights when an airplane flies into a storm or in or out of a jet stream.

# FURTHER READING

## Books

Ivancic, Linda. *What Is Wind?* New York, NY: Cavendish Square Publishing, 2016.

Orr, Tamra B. *The Wind Blows.* Ann Arbor, MI: Cherry Lake Publishing, 2015.

Tomas, Isabel. *Wind: Explore, Create and Investigate.* London, UK: QED Publishing, 2016.

VanVoorst, Jenny. *Wind.* Minneapolis, MN: Jump, 2016.

## WEBSITES

**PBS, Inside the Jet Stream**
*www.pbs.org/wgbh/nova/earth/inside-the-jet-stream.html*
Go on an interactive tour of a jet stream.

**Weather Wiz Kids, Wind**
*www.weatherwizkids.com/weather-wind.htm*
**Dive deeper into the subject of wind.**

**Wonderpolis, What Is a Jet Stream?**
*wonderopolis.org/wonder/what-is-a-jet-stream*
Read more facts about jet streams.

# INDEX